Clarence J. Selby

Flashes of Light from an Imprisoned Soul

Clarence J. Selby

Flashes of Light from an Imprisoned Soul

ISBN/EAN: 9783744762243

Printed in Europe, USA, Canada, Australia, Japan

Cover: Foto ©Thomas Meinert / pixelio.de

More available books at **www.hansebooks.com**

FLASHES OF LIGHT ✟ ✟ ✟ ✟ ✟ FROM AN IMPRISONED SOUL.

BY CLARENCE J. SELBY.

1895.

A. L. FYFE, PRINTER AND PUBLISHER,

334 DEARBORN STREET,

CHICAGO.

PREFACE.

Although I had seen Clarence Selby and talked with him at the Le Couteulx Deaf Mute Institution in Buffalo, N. Y., and had seen him often, after he came to Chicago to reside with his parents, it was with delight as well as surprise that I read the pages of the manuscript, which he had composed and printed on his small pin-prick frame. It was a model of neatness and of accuracy as to its mechanical execution, and what vivacity, what a flow of language and still more of ideas! At once I realized what had been the motive of his book, which was to put himself in communication with his fellow-men, by expressing what was in his heart and mind; sentiments, impressions which he had longed in vain to utter in his isolation, until his soul ached for sympathizing listeners. With this realization came, also, a reverent consciousness of the richness of the human mind, depending, in many ways, upon it surroundings but still possessing within itself eternal springs of thought, an eternal flow of images. I realized also, that it was the natural desire to communicate these thoughts and images to those around him— not only to receive from them but to share his own treasures with them—which had given a strange joy and a strange anguish to his isolated, shut in life. The desire for knowledge which pursued him, notwithstanding the limited conditions under which it could be acquired, was another proof of the innate powers of the human soul, so that the manuscript was not only a narrative of a youth deprived of two such sources of knowledge and happiness as sight and hearing, but a psychological revelation of the complex human being.

To suppose that his descriptions of scenes which he had never beheld, are mere reproductions of the descriptions written on his hand by the light touch of the Sister to whom he expresses himself as so deeply indebted for her patience—which should be named enthusiastic patience—or the companionship of his mother who is to him both sight and hearing, is impossible. There is a freshness of fancy, an incisiveness of detail, a stretch of the imagination, which show that the descriptions given to him by the Sister or his mother, touched a spark within his own mind, lighting up a picture which few would describe so vividly even if blessed with sight.

It is not, therefore, so much to the compassion of his readers that our young author appeals, as to their sensibility and their sympathy. No one can read these pages without a deeper wish than ever, that the instructors of the deaf, the dumb, the blind, all those deprived of all these precious senses, may not only be rewarded for their enthusiastic patience in teaching their charges, but may find their own inventiveness quickened so as to discover new ways of communication between themselves and their pupils, and thus lead to still more effectual methods of instruction, facilitating the intercourse between those deprived of these beautiful senses and their more favored fellow beings.

This leads me, quite naturally, to speak of the Ephpheta School for Deaf Mutes at 409 May Street, Chicago. From the inception of this school in the mind of the ardent Redemptorist, Father Maurer, the placing of the pupils under the care of the Sisters of the Holy Heart of Mary, to the present time, every step has been marked with a special blessing. Never has a child been refused a place in the school, in the dormitory or the refectory because of the lack of means, on the part of its parents to defray the expenses, and often the clothing has been supplied, and the yearly exhibits of the class work, of hand work in sewing, modelling in clay, wood carving, drawing and painting, prove how far-seeing is the policy of the Superiors in providing various occupations for their pupils; while the dramas in pantomime which they perform, proves that the ideality of the pupils is fostered and directed. These pantomimes, founded sometimes on historical events, like the victory of Constantine, or charming ideals of virtue, are produced with a brilliancy altogether marvelous, unless we concede that a certain intensity is often the result of the deprivation of a sense; and to all this we must add the unaffected piety fostered by these religious ladies among their pupils. Under the influence of this education, both intellectual and religious, the desert of life, as it must have been to many before entering this lovely institution, blossoms as the rose, and brings forth all the happy fruits of knowledge and of virtue.

Most fervently may we all pray Almighty God to bless all such institutions throughout the land in which He is honored; and most fervently too, we may pray that many a legacy and bequest may increase the always too limited means of these charitable institutions, in order that they may be able to give more and more generous opportunities to their pupils for acquiring knowledge; and also be encouraged to pursue elegant and artistic handicrafts requiring time for their acquisition.

It is therefore, not only for the sake of our young author, Clarence Selby, that we desire the success of this little book, but in behalf of all deaf, mute, blind or crippled children, and of all in any way deprived of the unspeakable blessing of perfect senses in a healthy body.

ELIZA ALLEN STARR.

Saint Joseph's Cottage.
Feast of Our Lady of Good Counsel,
1897.

DEDICATION.

To Sister M. Dosetheus:

My kind guide, instructor and friend, I dedicate the following pages. I humbly lay at your feet, the first branch plucked from the tree of knowledge, by you implanted in my mind, after many years of patient labor, unflagging zeal, and interest, in what must have appeared a barren soil. May it become a tree so vast, so luxuriant, that all around it may feel its influence and be benefitted therefrom, which is the earnest wish of your most grateful former pupil.

CLARENCE J. SELBY.

FLASHES OF LIGHT

FROM AN IMPRISONED SOUL.

WILL now give a brief sketch of my life. I was born in the year 1872, in a pretty little village on the east coast of England. But owing to the fact of my father's failure in business, he left England for America bringing his family with him, when I was about three years of age; consequently I can remember but little of my native land. We settled in New York state and there I passed a few years of most exquisite happiness, for at that time I enjoyed the precious gifts of sight and hearing of which I am now deprived. But I am thankful to God for granting me even that brief space of time, for I retain the pleasant remembrance of scenery and places, which often cheer many a lonely hour now that I cannot see. I attended a public school for a few months and soon learned to read and spell, when I became afflicted with a disease of the optic nerves which was very painful and prevented my studying or using my eyes in any way. I was attended by the best physicians and everything was done for me that was in their power to do; but in spite of their efforts my sight failed me and I became blind, then after suffering another three months the most acute pain in my ears, I lost my hearing. Since that time I have lived in an ideal world of my own, for while shut out from the sights and sounds of much that is good and beautiful I am spared from listening to the wicked and dreadful things that are around us.

My first grief came to me when death snatched away from us my darling little brother Willie, at the age of three years and three months. He was the youngest in the family, a pretty blue-eyed fair-haired child, his long curls floated in the wind as he ran and played in the garden. He was beloved by all, and his death was so sudden that it was a terrible blow for us. He only lived a few hours from the time he was first seized with convulsions.

I think my sister Ada grieved more than the rest of us, she was two years older than him, his constant playmate, and she missed him, oh! so much. They buried him in a small cemetery near our home, and whenever we missed Ada we soon knew where we would find her, for at every opportunity she would slip away and cover the little grave with flowers.

Time passed slowly with me then, not being able to see or hear what was going on around me. In spite of the fact that every one around me tried their best to amuse me and make my life as pleasant as possible, I was not satisfied; I wanted to study, my mind was craving for knowledge. My mother bought me a box of blocks with raised letters on them and I could form words and spell with them but that was too slow. She then wrote to Dr. Wilbur of Batavia, New York state, asking that I might be admitted to his Institution for the blind. Upon her stating that I was deaf as well as blind, he wrote back that he could not receive me, but kindly forwarded some books in raised letters so that I could commence learning to read them at home.

Shortly after this a kind friend of ours who was then a Superintendent of an Asylum in Newark, Wayne County, came to visit us. He kindly wrote to the Superintendent of the St. Mary le Coreteulx Deaf Mute Institute, in Buffalo, New York state, who, becoming anxious to see me and find out if I could be taught, sent for me to come to her. My father at once took me to Buffalo, and after examining me and finding that my mind was clear, and intellect keen, she decided that I should remain there, and that Sister Dosetheus should take charge of me and educate me. Words can never express my gratitude to that dear, kind, patient Sister who devoted so many days and weeks teaching me individually. Accustomed as she was to educating the deaf mutes who depend in a great measure upon their eyesight, it was a double task to teach me without sight or hearing and depending entirely upon the sense of touch. My mind under her constant care began to unfold, and I not only learned to read and write, but I gained much valuable information from the books of both ancient and modern history which she kindly read to me whenever she had leisure.

I suppose you will imagine it was strange that she should read to me being unable to see or hear her, but the system was this: Spelling the words with her fingers as is the custom of the deaf mutes, I placed my hand over hers and as she formed each letter my sense of touch enabled me to understand, and I soon learned to grasp the meaning of each word however rapidly she might read.

My life at school was a very pleasant one, each and all of the Sisters were so kind to me and did all that lay in their power to make me happy. I wrote and received many letters both from my home and other places, and I had many friends and acquaintances in Buffalo, who often paid me a visit, bringing me little gifts and keepsakes which I prize very much.

On the 10th of August, 1889, a small party of school boys, myself included, accompanied by two of our teachers left the Couteulx Institution, Buffalo, to spend a week among the pretty little hills and valleys of Portage, New York. This pleasure was owing to an invitation from the Hon. W. P. Letchworth, a distinguished gentleman who owns a large and most beautiful estate called Glen-Iris, delightfully situated on the banks of the Genesee River. Upon our arrival at a small place called Castile, we found a young man awaiting us with a carryall drawn by three lovely horses, so we soon stepped into the vehicle and were rapidly driven over the beautiful hills and through the bracing air of Portage, to the beautiful home of our kind host who received us with a most hearty wel-

come—and Glen-Iris—I cannot find words to describe
its loveliness. Not only the mansion itself filled us
with admiration, but the surroundings were so harmonious, everything was so artistic. Scattered here
and there were pretty cottages and grand stables for
the beautiful horses—groves of fine trees, orchards of
the finest fruit, fields of grain, herds and flocks of fine
cattle. Parks, lawns, and miniature lakes, flowers,
shrubs and fountains, every device that art could sug-
gest to assist nature. Two days after our arrival, two
of the Sisters came on from Buffalo, and how delighted
I was to meet them; for one was my teacher, and
through her kindness I was able to enjoy and appreciate all the pleasures of our visit.

She described each beautiful scene to me so that
I could see it plainly in my imagination. She would
laughingly tell me she would lend me her eyes and
ears for a time, which was certainly correct for she
would tell me of all that was going on around me in
such a delightful manner that I seemed to see and
hear it all as plainly as she did herself, so sympathetic
and harmonious were our natures. And right here let
me add that thought transference is not as some people
believe, a fad, but a reality which can be clearly proven;

for it has not only been transmitted to me by the one person, but others, whom I have come in contact with whose natures were perfectly harmonious with my own.

One day we visited an old building that stood without the grounds that had been formerly used as a council house by the red men, where they had held their treaties; we entered it and found there were articles and objects of interest that had formerly belonged to the Indians, and which I was allowed to examine. In the adjacent grounds were three cannons lying on the ground, one of them being a large British cannon. About 1771 when the Indians held their council, this cannon was fired by a British soldier. It was about ten feet in length; thirty of the Indians were there and when the gun was fired they all jumped up two feet from the ground. I said it must have been a wonderful jump; sixty feet for thirty Indians. Mr. Letchworth saw the joke and laughed heartily at it. After spending seven happy days in that most delightful place, we returned to Buffalo with feelings of the greatest gratitude to the Hon. W. P. Letchworth.

We then resumed our school duties. I had been presented with a ciphering case which contained raised figures by which means I was enabled to study arithmetic. I then received from Mother Mary Anne, our Superior, a nice pin type case with which I learned to write. I did not care so much for grammar or arithmetic, but I loved to study geography and all histories, both ancient and modern; so I have read Egyptian, Grecian and Roman history, also that of England, Ireland, Scotland, Wales, Peru and the United States.

I have also read natural history and many other books that are printed for the blind in raised letters. I love to read and write. I understand every method of speaking by hand used in the sign language by the deaf mutes. In addition to these methods my parents converse with me by writing on the back of my hand with their fingers, which I quickly understand. My kind teacher, Sister Dosetheus, made me a glove and fastened the alphabet in raised letters in the palm of it, so that when I meet strangers who wish to speak with me and do not understand the sign language, I put on the glove and they spell the words to me by touching the letters. In this way when I travel alone, as I have often done, I always meet with kind people who interest themselves in me and I enjoy talking with them very much.

I do not feel so helpless as some people imagine, for I can do so many things to help myself, but have never learned a trade as I take more pleasure in writing and composition. I lie awake many hours at night rehearsing things in my mind, for that is the time when my thoughts are clearest. I remember several times when I was at school I used to drop off to sleep in class after being awake so many hours before; and the boys were very much amused to see me nodding and falling over. I dream a great deal and the most delightful dreams. I see lovely scenery and visit many places in my dreams; sometimes I see ancient castles and fortresses, at other times I seem in the tropics where the trees and plants are so large and so strange, and I see all kinds of wild beasts, birds and reptiles, some of them so frightful that they make me shudder; and then again I see good people that are now dead and I talk with them and often feel sorry when I awake from my dreams because then I can see and hear, but when I awake all is dark. My parents left the East for Chicago some time before I left school, so that I spent my vacations in Chicago with them. During the year of the World's Fair I left school having completed my education.

I must here tell you that I was received into the true Church about two months after I had passed my nineteenth birthday and received my first Communion, February 7, 1891.   I was confirmed by the Rev. S. V. Ryan, Bishop of Buffalo, who has since died.   Just before I left school I received a silver medal with my name engraved upon it as a token of good conduct from the hands of the Rev. P. S. Dunn, pastor of Le Couteulx Institute, who died soon afterwards.

After arriving in Chicago, I found nothing talked of but the World's Fair; everyone was anxious to go and see it, and I for one was as anxious as the rest.   So my mother took me there and I really did enjoy it very much, for as she described the things to me I seemed to see them and was kindly allowed to touch several things.   I will now proceed to tell you some things about it.

Jackson Park, which is beautifully located on the shores of Lake Michigan, in the great city of Chicago, was taken for the World's Exposition in 1893, to cele-brate the 400th anniversary of the Discovery of America by Christopher Columbus.   The park contains about six hundred and thirty-three acres of ground entirely level.   When it was taken for exposition purposes, it is stated that seventy-four million feet of lumber and twenty thousand tons of iron and steel were used in the erection of its numerous magnificent buildings. One immense structure covered an area of forty-four acres, and another covered seventeen acres.

On September 8th, during one of my visits to the World's Fair, accompanied by my mother, I went through a number of large stables where hundreds of fine horses were shown. There were ponies and donkeys also. I was allowed to feel of the animals, among them were several pretty little ponies, nice donkeys, and ever so many horses. I examined the Czar's beautiful horses. One was a black horse with a fine arched neck; he held his head up and looked as if he wanted to say, "Look at me, I belong to a royal family!" His beautiful blankets with the Czar's name on them, were hanging near him. A gentleman took me to see the largest horse of all. It was an English horse of a light color and weighed over a ton. A horseman gave me a book containing the pictures of the best horses. We then went to see the cattle. There were all sorts of fine cattle to be seen; among them a number of hornless cattle and a pretty pair of twin calves. At one of the stables I got acquainted with a gentleman who had in his possession some beautiful black Aberdeen cattle, and I think a great many Holstein, Durham, Jersey, Aberdeen, and little Brittany cattle. After we had spent some time going through these immense stables and evening was approaching, we left them.

Afterward we went through several other immense buildings, viz: the Transportation, Mining, Electricity, and other buildings. In the Transportation building I was very much interested, for all sorts of vehicles were on exhibition. I examined three of the largest locomotives, one was from Philadelphia, one was from Pittsburgh and the third was an English one. Besides I looked over several of the Brooks' locomotives from Dunkirk, New York. They seemed very fine. I also examined boats and many other things.

At the Mining building, all sorts of mineral products and natural objects were to be seen. There were two huge blocks, one of iron and one of coal, which were obtained from the Pennsylvania mines. In the Electricity building many kinds of machines, lights and articles were shown. Cooking, baking, picture-making and egg-hatching were done by means of electricity. As the sun had disappeared from sight and it was getting late, we left the great exposition grounds and on one of the long streets entered the Manitoba Hotel, where we examined a fine collection of stuffed animals, birds, etc. We then took a car to the elevated line for home which was reached at half-past nine o'clock.

I think you will agree with me that the day was pleasantly and profitably spent.

When the railroad men had their celebration at the Exposition grounds there was a very pretty parade and everything looked nice there. All sorts of vehicles passed along to show every manner of riding, and what could be more beautiful than the beautiful boats sailing about on the lake. The whole scene was grand.

Locomotives, different kinds of cars, and pretty carriages passed along in the procession. People were mounted on camels, horses and donkeys. A grand carriage was drawn by the Czar's fine horses. The Turks, Japanese and Javanese took part in the parade. They carried queer looking things called Sedan chairs, and palanquins, in which persons were seated. Two Indians carried a funny looking thing on their shoulders with an Indian woman seated on it. An Esquimaux with sledge and reindeer drove along. The last thing in the procession was a very handsome baby-carriage with a little child in it.   The little one seemed very merry.   It was smiling and with its tiny hands threw kisses to the people.   They laughed and cheered and threw kisses in return to the little thing.

During the evening there was a grand display of fireworks.   A clever German performed some very daring feats on a wire which was attached to two high buildings.   He walked along on the wire, turned over, then stood and sent up fireworks.   He was very daring and the people looked on with surprise.

On October 9, when the grand celebration in memory of the great Chicago fire took place, about three quarters of a million people are said to have gathered on the grounds.   During the evening a scene was enacted showing an old cow kicking over a lantern smashing it and setting the place in a blaze.

At that time I had two dear sisters; one was two years younger than myself but taller, and she had lovely dark eyes and hair.   I can remember how she used to look when I could see.   The other was a bright little girl ten years younger than the oldest; she had pretty blue eyes and long fair hair in curls.   Oh, how I loved them both! for they were very kind to me.

The eldest was employed during the day so that she could not devote much time to me, but the little one, my favorite, was like a little wingless angel. She was possessed of great knowledge although so young, she was my little guide, would conduct me safely through the busy streets as well as an older person would have done; she also took me to church and did all she could to make life pleasant for me. But, oh, how sad I feel! now my little angel guide has gone to join the other bright spirits above.

I am alone now, for cruel death snatched away both of my dear sisters within two weeks of each other, one year ago from typhoid fever. My eldest sister was received into the Church while at school at St. Peters' academy, Rome, N. Y., and the little one was receiving religious instructions in order to prepare her for baptism. She received much comfort and religious instruction from Mrs. Charles Moody, a most estimable lady who is a benevolent christian, and a lady of most lovely disposition. She was my little sister's kindest and best friend during her sickness and death. She was her godmother and cheered the poor little soul with words of love and comfort as she passed away; and then after she was dead sent a beautiful cross of

flowers, that almost covered the little white casket with
their luxuriant leaves and blossoms, and filled the air
with their fragrance. Father Therein was her spiritual
adviser, she was baptized three days before she died
and such a happy death was hers, so peaceful that all
those who were with her said if they could die such a
happy death what a good thing it would be. When
my sisters were taken sick the kind Sisters at Buffalo
wrote to me to come to them at once in order to relieve
my mother of some of her cares. I went, but on the
day of my little sister's death I was taken sick with the
fever and the kind Sisters so kindly nursed me through
it that I can never forget them nor repay them for
the time and trouble they spent with me. I staid with
them until the following June, then I returned to
Chicago, where I have remained ever since.

I pass my time reading, or I write compositions
some of which are published in *Le Couteulx Leader,* a
magazine printed by the deaf mutes in Buffalo, New
York. I will now give an account of my visit to Lincoln Park.

Lincoln Park, so-called in honor of one of our
good presidents, Abraham Lincoln, is one of the most
beautiful parks in Chicago, and is nicely situated on

the shore of Lake Michigan, at the north side of the city. It covers an area of two hundred and ninety-five acres, and is filled with trees, flower beds, lagoons, several fountains and many other things for amusement and sport.

There are several large structures for the confinement of animals, birds and water creatures. Among the fierce animals are lions, tigers, leopards, a pair of jaguars, a puma, a small collection of bears, and several wolves, coyotes and wild cats; some large animals are also to be seen there; for instance, an elephant, several buffalos, different kinds of deer, and a pair of llamas. Among the water animals are sea lions, seals, beavers, the little gila monsters, alligator and otter.

Besides these there are many smaller animals, such as foxes, badgers, raccoons, prairie-dogs, and quite a collection of monkeys. There are several collections of birds consisting of parrots, owls, pigeons, some kind of water-fowl and many other odd birds.

Near one of the driveways in the park stands a colossal bronze statue of Abraham Lincoln, and a little way from it stands a statue of General Grant and his horse. By paying fifty cents you may have one of the little ponies and a carriage for an hour to drive around the pretty grounds and view the delightful scenery. The lagoons are furnished with little boats for merry boating.

When I first returned to Chicago, I thought I might be able to learn a trade as there is an institution for the blind established near Douglas Park. I put in a formal application for admission to the superintendent of it, but when I went to him he refused to admit me, because from the fact of my being blind it would be too much trouble for them to teach me the trade of broom making which is carried on there. I was very much disappointed at not being received into the institution as I could very easily have learned it had the superintendent been disposed to admit me.

But I will now tell you a little more about the school where I passed so many happy years, for I shall always remember them with feelings of the greatest pleasure and gratitude. Could people only know the self-sacrificing lives that those kind Sisters live, shut in from the rest of the world, teaching the deaf mutes, many of whom are very obstinate and difficult to manage and some so ignorant that they do not know one word, but are soon taught not only to read but to write and to understand what they read and to have a knowledge of things in general. Upon entering the school a deaf mute is first shown a card on which the deaf mute alphabet is printed, and are taught to form letters with their hands, they are then taught to spell, then taken to a room called the museum which is filled with models of things in general use. The teacher shows them an article, then teaches them to spell the name of it so they can call it by name; then they are shown what the article is used for and when they are still further advanced they are taught to draw it, and also to write a composition about it. In this way they are able to obtain a knowledge of things in general, and go through the different grades the same as scholars in other schools.

The girls are also taught to sew and do all kinds of fancy work, or whatever they are best adapted for. The boys learn the carpenter work, printing, tailoring, shoemaking and caning chairs, and many other useful occupations, so that when they leave school they become self-supporting. Some of them are remarkably intelligent. The boys print a magazine called *Le Couteulx Leader*, and the scholars are taught to write short compositions to be inserted in it. One was written by a scholar about another little fellow who had just commenced to learn the names of objects, told how they showed him a small wheelbarrow, told him its name and showed him how to use it, they showed him how to fill it with erasers, then wheel it to another place and unload it. He got so much interested in his work he wanted to do it all the time. Another one upon being shown a straw hat learned its name and use. He did not want to take it off but wanted to wear it on his head all the time. They do many funny things that make people laugh at them.

During the time of the World's Fair I went to the Chicago University to meet Helen Keller, who is like myself, blind and deaf. Of course we could both speak, but neither of us could hear each other, so conversed in the language of the deaf mutes. She is a very intellectual young lady and well educated; I quite enjoyed my visit with her. Taking all things in consideration I think I enjoy my life as well as many people that can both hear and see. I try to be as happy as I can and I am consoled with this one bright thought, that ere many more years are passed and gone, I, too shall pass away and shall be with those I love, where there will be no more blindness, deafness, sorrow, or pain, but an endless eternity of happiness and peace.

I will now tell you a little about Buffalo. It is a fine place in the western part of the state of New York, and is nicely situated on the shore of Lake Erie. Its population is over two hundred thousand and it is noted for its railroads. The Niagara River flows near by it and the Erie canal starts from the great lake there. St. Mary le Couteulx Institution for the deaf mutes at Buffalo, is nicely located on a very suitable slice of level ground in the upper part of the city and is in charge of the Sisters of St. Joseph. Rev. Mother Mary Anne is the Superior of this benevolent establishment. Rev. P. S. Gilmore is the pastor for the deaf mutes at present.

About the middle of the present century some time before the outbreak of the civil war, a man from France named le Couteulx, before his death gave a small tract of land to the city on purpose for the erection of a school for deaf mutes, besides which he left other ground for other edifices to be built upon. Very soon Bishop Timon, the first bishop of Buffalo, undertook the management of it and opened a small school which he placed in charge of the Catholic nuns. After some years had elapsed a fine large structure sprang up, where three hundred deaf mute children are

now gathered to receive instruction; the state also
appropriates a sum annually towards the support of it.
I am the only blind and deaf mute that ever received
an education there, my family being Protestant. They
of course tried to find some protestant institution to
have me taught in, but failing to do so placed me there,
so that if it had not been for the kindness of the
Catholic Sisters I should never have been educated and
should have to remain my life long, in darkness and
ignorance; whereas I am now educated and understand
all that is going on in the world almost as well as if I
had sight and hearing. Many Protestants that are
prejudiced against the Catholic religion say they were
surprised to think that my parents should place me in
the care of the Catholics. I asked them why they did
not follow the example of the Catholics and provide
suitable institutions for those that are afflicted, to be
educated in. Nowhere, among all their different creeds
and sects will you find any of them that will do what
those noble christian women of the Catholic Church
will do for poor suffering humanity, and I thank God
that through their kind influence I have become what
I am. My Sundays I generally pass in going to Mass
in the morning, and in the afternoon I visit the Eph-

pheta school, on May street, where lectures are given
by the priest to the deaf mutes. I am able to follow
the thread of his discourse through the kindness of a
lady, that is a Sister there who spells the words to me
with her fingers while I place my hand over hers and feel
the formation of each letter which she does very rapidy,
so that I can grasp the meaning as quickly as those
that can see, and I feel very grateful for her extreme
kindness. I will now give an account of this school:

The Catholic School for Deaf Mutes, of Chicago.

St. Joseph's Home, so called by the Sisters of the
Sacred Heart of Mary, is a convent school for deaf
mutes and is located on South May Street. In this
benevolent establishment about one hundred and fifty
children may gather to obtain instruction. Miss
Coughlin is the Superior of the establishment, and
Miss M. C. Hendrick is the Superintendent. About
thirteen years ago, Miss Hendrick, who had been a
teacher for some years at St. Joseph's convent, at Ford-
ham, New York, left New York for Chicago, accompanied by several teachers for the purpose of opening
a school for the deaf. She well knew that a large

number of deaf and dumb children of Catholic parents
were to be found in this city, that were in much need
of a christian education. Here these good Sisters
opened a school where they obtained quite a number
of pupils, consisting of both boys and girls.   Here
the good Sisters have spent many happy years doing
their good work that will bring them lasting glory.

The place consists of several buildings on a small
area of level ground, in the main building, there is a
chapel where a Jesuit Father celebrates Mass every
morning.   At St. Joseph's school I often meet the deaf
mutes on Sunday, for the pleasure of hearing the beautiful sermons and instructions delivered by the holy
priest.   Those sermons are always explained to me by
a dear little Sister, named Miss Gethings, who is very
conversant in the sign language.   Now, I have just
written this little sketch of the Catholic school for the
deaf, but I will here write a little more.   The little
band of Sisters at the convent at present, are doing all
in their power to cause a fine new school to be erected
in a better situation, and are in hopes that they may
soon be able to take possession of a fine new establishment.

Now, it would please me in the highest degree if these good teachers can be successful in their good plans, and I hope that a large, new institution for the deaf and dumb of Chicago, may be opened before long, as I dearly love little children and am quite anxious to become some day a teacher myself.

My Visit to the McCowen Oral School for Little Deaf Children.

On Thursday last, I received an invitation to attend the closing exercises of the Oral School for young deaf children, at 6550 Yale avenue, this city, which I gladly accepted, as I am always delighted to visit any school where the deaf or otherwise afflicted are taught. In company with my mother we took the Wentworth avenue car to 63d street, then alighted, and walked down Yale avenue to the school. How much I enjoyed the clear bracing atmosphere, how different to that of the city; the beautiful shade trees and shrubs, and the lovely lawns of green grass, all smelled so sweet and fragrant. They seemed to inspire me with new life. Upon arriving at the school which is a lovely residence, standing in the midst of a green lawn surrounded with trees and shrubs. We were met at the door by a young lady who conducted us through numerous halls and corridors to the class room where we were met and cordially welcomed by Miss Emma M. Firth, one of the teachers, a young lady I esteem very highly. She introduced us to several ladies who had assembled there to witness the closing exercises, and showed me a great many articles made by the little ones carved in wood, such as inkstands, match strikers, pencil sharpeners, sponge holders, ribbon winders, and many other things too numerous to mention. The walls were hung with drawings and paintings; and various articles are also represented, their shapes being cut out in colored paper and pasted on cardboard, all of which were made by the hands of the dear little ones. A lady kindly sang some pretty songs, then the little ones went through their various exercises; one with the dumb bells was excellent, also march and counter marching and dancing, besides games played by the little tots of three and four years of age, and just imagine all this is done by watching the motion of the teacher's lips as she speaks, for not one can hear—and as I sat there feeling the sound of the little feet as they danced or marched, how much I wished that for the sake of such dear little ones I could be rich. How I would seek

out such afflicted ones and place them in schools like
this, where they might be educated and become talented
men and women. If the rich people would only visit
these schools and see for themselves, I know they would
gladly forego some of their frivolous and extravagant
pleasures for the greater pleasure of knowing that
they had benefited some poor, afflicted child by bestow-
ing upon them some of the money wasted needlessly.
Of course I can sympathize with the dear little ones
more than others, as I am afflicted the same myself.

After the exercises were over refreshments were
handed to the visitors by the little pupils. I then met
Mme. M. McCowen, the Principal, and I was delighted
with her for she is a very bright and talented lady;
she kindly invited us to stay to supper with her and
what a pleasant meal it was! two lovely connecting
dining rooms with four large tables bountifully spread
with choice food at which were seated both teachers
and pupils all engaged in pleasant conversation with
each other; no formality, just one happy family
grouped together. What a feeling of peace pervaded
the atmosphere. I felt the vibrations of perfect har-
mony surrounding me and knew that a blessing from
Heaven rested on that peaceful abode. After supper

by the means of my alphabet glove, I had a long conversation with Miss Rhea Freeman, a young lady who was educated in this school. I found her to be a very bright and intelligent young lady; I also conversed with several of the teachers. I thoroughly enjoyed my visit. Upon leaving, Miss Emma M. Firth kindly presented me with a lovely little book written by herself, entitled: "Stories of Old Greece," also a number of the magazine entitled: "The Little Deaf Child," which is edited by Miss McCowen and Miss Firth; both of which I appreciate very highly. Then after many kindly good-byes I started for home, delighted with my visit to the McCowen Oral School for Little Deaf Children. Long may it prosper is the fervent prayer of CLARENCE J. SELBY.

Professor N. Konshi, a well known gentleman of Tokyo, Japan, who is the director of the Imperial school for the blind and deaf of that remarkable city, has been spending some time in the United States, for the purpose of investigating the various methods of teaching the blind and deaf in this country. He has visited the schools of Chicago, Jacksonville, Washington and New York. He is going to Europe early this summer where he will remain for some time, from whence he will return to his beautiful home in Japan.

This jolly little Jap when traveling carries his cards with his name written upon them both in Japanese and English. He visits schools, printing houses, and many other places of interest. He closely examines all the machinery, and all apparatus used in the construction of books for the blind; also the different systems of writing.

Now I will tell you more about the Japanese Professor and what a great pleasure it was for me to have the opportunity of meeting him.

N. Konshi is small of stature and has black hair and whiskers, also black eyes, and he is so kind and has such a beautiful, gentle disposition. He understands several languages and writes the English language very nicely, although he is unable to speak it very fluently.

This distinguished gentleman has called upon me twice, and each time spent several hours with me. We talked together by spelling the words on my alphabet glove. He brought with him many cards, papers and different systems used in the instruction of the blind, all of which he kindly explained to me. He presented me the cards and papers containing the

French and Japanese as well as the English language, being the perfect system of instruction for learning to write the same in raised point print. He said he was very anxious to have me study these new methods. I then announced my intentions to him, saying, I am very willing and shall take the greatest pleasure studying these systems, for I wish to be able both to read and write all these languages perfectly, also to study all other raised systems that I come in contact with. I then thanked the Professor for his great kindness to me and acknowledged how much I appreciated the great love and sympathy he feels for myself and all other persons that are deprived of any of the precious gifts of sight, speech or hearing. He kindly requested me to regularly correspond with him during the time he is traveling, also when he returns to his Japanese home, and should I ever have the opportunity to visit that lovely land, he has given me a cordial invitation to go and stay with him in his home, which I hope some day to do, and by the Professor have the honor of an introduction to His Imperial Majesty, the Mikado of Japan, who like the Professor is greatly interested in all things pertaining to the afflicted.

CLARENCE J. SELBY.

A BUTTERFLY.

A gay little butterfly rose with the sun,
  "Ha, ha," said he, "I will have some fun,"
"I will wile away the morning hours
  Flirting with the dear little flowers."

Then merrily he began to sing,
  As he shook the dust from his beautiful wing,
And washed his face with a dew-drop fair
  That sparkled on a rose-leaf there.

"And now, I am ready to start," said he,
  "I feel as happy as can be,"
So, away he darted through the air,
  In and among the flowers so rare.

A stately white lily lowered her head,
  And all around her fragrance shed;
He ventured, just to peep in her eye
  And beat his breast and began to sigh.

But she looked at him with such disdain,
  He dared no longer there remain,
So he concluded away he would fly,
  And courteously bowing, said, "good-bye."

To the little blue-bells he kisses threw,
  Who laughed and said, "we are ashamed of you,"
But merrily shook their heads in fun,
  Said he, " you are coquettes, every one."

When he flattered the pansies they opened their eyes,
  And gazed at him with great surprise,
No matter how subtly he wielded his art,
  He could not win a pansy's heart.

A tiny rosebud grew by the side
  Of her mother rose, that had opened wide;
He snatched a kiss from the rosebud's cheek,
  And she too frightened was to speak.

The mother would not such insult brook;
  With indignation she fairly shook,
Till her beautiful petals fell to the ground,
  Scattering their fragrance all around.

And when he saw the mischief he had done,
  He merely said, "I was only in fun,"
So he spread his wings and away he flew
  To amuse himself in pastures new.

And so he passed the bright sunny hours,
  Visiting numbers of beautiful flowers,
Admiring the young and flattering the old;
  Some laughed, some cried, some said he was bold.

The sun was sinking in the west,
  "I am tired," said he, "I'll go to rest;
I'll under the leaf of that Holly-bush creep,"
  And very soon he was fast asleep.

A REPLY.

Many a one has asked this question:
"Can you any pleasure find?
Your life must be so sad and lonely
Since you are both deaf and blind,"
Sad and lonely—No, indeed!
Could I but to them impart
Half the peaceful, joyous pleasures
That are stored within my heart.

Instead of pitying they would envy;
Could they those bright visions see
Scenes of wondrous heavenly beauty
God so kindly sends to me;
And the sounds of sweetest music
Ring upon my inward ear
Angel voices, sweet, harmonious,
Softly chanting I can hear.

None can know the peaceful feeling
That pervades my inmost breast,
Knowing that my Heavenly Father
Gives to me what He thinks best.
If I had my sight and hearing
With earth I might contented be,
Never thinking of God's Heaven
And its joys in store for me.

So I praise my Heavenly Father,
Who will guide me with His hand
O'er earth's rough and stormy journey,
To that bright and happy land.
When I reach those blissful portals
My prisoned soul will then be free ;
In that land of light and beauty
I shall ever hear and see.

www.ingramcontent.com/pod-product-compliance
Lightning Source LLC
Chambersburg PA
CBHW021442090426
42739CB00009B/1602